Living V.I.T.A.L
From Adversity to Advantage

Living V.I.T.A.L

From Adversity to Advantage

Andre St. George

4-U-Nique Publishing
A Series of VLB/VBJ Enterprises, LLC

INTRODUCTION

In this book, I outline events and situations that I have faced in my life and how the process of living V.I.T.A.L became the very tool I used to overcome wanting to throw in the towel and give up, to become the inspirational influence that has helped future young leaders strive to live extraordinary lives. It is no coincidence that I have travelled this road I'm on. There's no unseen "luck" attached to my name. I have experienced a boatload of failures and the outcomes were prevalent to the hardships many face in society today.

The one thing that has always set me apart is my will. My will to keep going, will to take risks, will to succeed, to never give up, will to believe I am destined for more. It is because of my will, backed by the process to achieve something better, I have been able to accomplish things most would only dream of. Granted, I have not made it yet but the fact that I am still moving and not standing still has given me the faith needed to keep going.

My hope is for you to read this and find that powerful source within you that keeps you going. That powerful source helps you to overcome adversity while transitioning you to a place where you are living a fulfilled life. I encourage you to take into account the many exercises at the end of the chapters that require you to put your thoughts on paper. Reading your written thoughts can give off a sense of entitlement to propel you forward in achieving the things you said you wanted in your life. Whether you are a teenager just starting your journey or an adult who has been traveling already, I will share with you what has helped me along the way. It was something I once read that said: "Give life to all that you have learned". This was so powerful to me that I wrote it on an index card and I now carry it with me wherever I go. Whenever I learn something new, I give life to it and in turn, it helps me to develop and grow in areas where I may be weak. My prayer is that it does the same for you.

Table of Contents

CHAPTER 1

(Always say "yes" to the present moment and surrender to what is. Say yes to life and see how life starts working for you rather than against you.)

Have you ever said "YES" to life? Where does a person find the courage to say yes to life? Society has shown us it is far easier to just say no and conform to the negative and controlling thoughts the word "No" produces. Being one of the shortest yet most powerful words in our vocabulary studies show that growing up a child hears the word no more than 400 times a day! That's extreme when you think about it but think about how that becomes a negative influence ingrained into a child's mind as they grow into adults which can hold them back. I was very curious as a child and my mother would tell me "no" one time, "don't do that". That was enough for me because I learned early on that the next "no" was usually followed by a pop on the hand or a spank on the butt, so I knew not to do it again.

The pattern of learning what-not-to-do have been set since an early age and as a parent, without knowing it, one can negatively impact a child just by the words that are spoken. A constant "no" is a parent's way of diminishing harm or the instinct a parent has to keep their child safe, but what it does is hurt the developing and building of self-esteem and can garner negative self-talk once a child becomes a teenager. This can even follow them once they transition into adulthood.

It takes great courage to find something meaningful and positive about our lives every day and by saying yes you create a continuous process of experiences that will empower you. I did not find my YES until later on, but when I did my life changed dramatically because I now had something that drove me to get out of bed every day. I was listening to a speech by Eric Thomas, and I hope you know who ET is, well in his speech he says stop waking up like its accident and start waking up knowing what you want. I meet people from all walks of life, young and old who still have no idea what they want to do in life. They are not sure about their dreams, nor do they see themselves doing anything other than what is currently comfortable to them right now. I find that type of life to be mundane, doing the same things day in and day out. Not having any fulfilment to look forward to or excitement to look back on, what if you have kids or plan to have kids one day and they inherit the same things where they don't say YES to life and never get to experience living outside of the box.

In my 20's I was able to visit other countries abroad and experience sky diving, not to mention riding a camel in the desert but all because I said YES to life. There is still so much more to do and accomplish and I do not plan on stopping anytime soon. But this is not about me though this is more about you and believing that those things are readily available for you.

I found it to be true that your circumstances do not make you, but they do reveal you to yourself. I've been through more than enough changes in my life and will continue to go through changes. But what happens is you find better ways to deal with life, as a result, I've become stronger mentally, I'm able to connect more spiritually, and I'm also able to grow and develop into a person others now admire and follow because I'm now walking in my purpose.

Let me tell you though it takes time and it is in that time most give up because they are expecting the overnight process to take effect. I have not made it yet, but I certainly am not the person I was when I first started. There is a process that comes with everything in life. If you like to cook there is a process to prepare food. If you lift weights, there is a process to building muscle. If you want to be successful there's a process one must follow to think differently. These are the rules to the game and if you follow the process there is no doubt that the things you want to happen will start to take shape in your life.

You will find throughout this book the changes I have made and how I used the process of living

V.I.T.A.L to get to where I am today; speaking on stages and even becoming an author. I want for you to start dreaming again and have a desire to do something greater than your current circumstances. Doing so will develop your story which can positively impact someone else that may be watching you and thinking to themselves that the life they're living now is all they will ever experience. I encourage you to make a plan for the next 21 days to wake up a little earlier than you have been doing. In waking up, before you do anything else, start your day by giving thanks for the opportunity you have for today. Next, walk into the bathroom or anywhere you have a mirror and repeat to yourself..."I am everything I need to be, I have the ability to do everything I need to do, I have the desire to live the life I am destined to live". I believe in you and because you inspire me, I am inspired to walk with you on this journey, now let's get this process started!

CHAPTER 2

The definition for the word V.I.T.A.L is read as "absolutely necessary or important; essential". Hearing those words just fires me up! I had a smile on my face while reading this. In doing so it got me thinking about my life right now and I had to ask myself the question am I truly living what one would call a V.I.T.A.L life? Am I doing what is absolutely necessary to live out my desires or my passion? Am I doing what is important to become the person I need to be now; not the person I was? Am I doing what is essential to make sure I stay on track and stay committed to my promise?

No one ever said the journey was going to be a brisk walk through the park. The pitfalls and potholes and everything else you will encounter along the way has been built to make it harder than anything you have ever faced. There is a survival instinct in us that was designed to make sure we prevail. Ever been in a situation where something was taken from you and you had to carry on despite the fact, or your back was against the wall and you had to make a reactive decision? If so, you know which instinct I'm talking about, it's that "survival mode" instinct. I started searching and found this to be true. After I heard a speaker say this at an event the light bulb immediately went off. See, no matter what, it will always revert to our training.

You were naturally born to survive. If you take a look at your parents (mother, father or both) and take into account how you were raised, then you will see they were leaders by example. They survived through a great deal to raise us; I make sure I tell my mother "thank you" all the time. But to take things a step deeper look at the definition of the word V.I.T.A.L that I outlined at the beginning. What is absolutely necessary, important, and essential begins to take shape and make you think of the word survival.

This book is the catalyst to get you started. If it wasn't for me going through some of the many adversities I've faced in my life I don't think I would have found what I was most passionate about. Being able to inspire those who inspire me has been a game-changer, especially once I figured out that was the very thing I was good at.

We have all been given gifts and talents and when used fervently the result is usually for the betterment of someone else. Think about the last person who entertained you, inspired you or motivated you to do, think, or feel better about yourself. Whoever that was, they understood their gifts and they used those gifts to change their own lives. You have that same ability to do so but, for some reason or another, you have not tapped into your potential yet. That very potential I'm referring to helps you understand what you can excel at and who you can become. The idea is to learn what makes you feel complete, what drives you to be the best version of you.

As I speak and share my story in front of audiences, I still remember a point in my life where even if you told me I would have never believed any of this to be possible. What can I say, I was a sceptic. I doubted any and everything and I know it came from a lack of confidence in myself.

Even the thought of writing a book was few and far between. The bright idea came to me about 2 years ago when I imagined what it would feel like to become a published author. It instantaneously became one of my goals but, because I stood in my way, I came up with every excuse. This resulted in never getting around to writing it. Do not get me wrong, I was not always procrastinating. I would do a little something here and there, but we all know that activity (being busy) does not necessarily mean accomplishment.

They say once you commit to a plan the universe will start to conform to your actions. Getting started, I found a bunch of old notebooks throughout the house where I had penciled in different thoughts, stories, and quotes, but never really sat down and put them all together. I believe my crutch was always debating with myself, thinking "if I wrote the book would it be readable? Would it inspire someone, or would it just be a dust collector?"

Too many times I hear people talk about being busy but never really accomplish anything. Whew, talk about bringing up my number one pet peeve. I see it like this, stop "letting presumption stop production" we must stop thinking about what someone might say or not approve of before we even make a move to do anything. You see I say we because I can talk about it. I have been victim to it more than once.

As I was thinking about that I realized, I have something to share and to even take it a step further I have a set of principles I followed to share as well. I first learned that there is a two-part process when talking about change. The first part of the process is awareness, what are you being aware of? Are you aware of your resources, are you aware of your numbers, are you aware of who you need to become? If you can answer yes to any of those questions, then I would say you are pretty aware, although that is the easy part. The awareness although being easy can sometimes be overlooked; I think we have all done it to some degree.

There is a difference in being aware of something and being aware to it. I was aware of the fact I was financially broken, but I was not aware to how to change the scenario. It was so embarrassing to reach down in that drawer and pull out that bag of change, holding it in my hand I turned it upside down and poured all the change out onto the bed. As I'm sifting through looking at how many quarters and dimes, I can put together do you know all I could come up with was $6! At the time a gallon of gas was 2.73, I had to get to work so took that change and went to the gas station.

Right before I went in, I waited for the line to go down so that no one would be behind me. As I get to the clerk I start laughing and apologize for all this change to kind of throw things off. The clerk looks at me and says don't worry about it as if she knew my situation I smile backed and said 6 on number 5 please and left out. My walk back to my car was the longest walk I've ever taken simply because it was a walk of shame and confusion.

See, it is easy to be aware, but it is not as easy to accept and implement change, and that brings me to the second part which is acceptance. I was pretty aware that I needed a change in my life, but I was clueless as to what I needed to accept to make that change. I knew I had not fully accepted not having my father in my life but being a father myself I just hid those feelings of anger and resentment. I thought I had already accepted dropping out of college and being somewhat of a disappointment to my mother, but again all I did was mask those emotions as well and buried them deep inside while still telling myself a lie that I accepted it. I thought I had already accepted my wrongs so there was nothing to use as a crutch for my excuses for not being the best me.

See for me it was always one adversity after another, what I did not know at the time and kind of found out later was that by accepting that adversity it allows you to change. I did not say it was going to make you change, it allows you to change but see I turned things around and mine went like this; the more I changed the less I accepted. I felt as if I did not have to accept anything I was walking away from.

I will give you a piece of advice and you can thank me later for this, having that negative type of mentality was not a good way to live. It quickly became how I acted in relationships, how I was with family and friends and even how I acted with my kids. There will be days when it seems like you are in a bad place and it feels like the whole world is against you, there is always a way out. I can honestly say that was probably the best advice I can give you simply because someone once gave the same advice to me. You're welcome!

CHAPTER 3

This basis of this book came from that statement alone. I know how it feels, I know what you are thinking, I know where you are because we've all been there so you're not alone. I can tell you this and you are smart so I'm sure you already know it's not going to be easy, but what is? I mean it's not easy growing up as a middle child, but I survived, and you will too. I got into personal development early on but it did not get into me until right around 2008-2009. And just like the typical story, I read Robert Kiyosaki's book "Rich Dad, Poor Dad" and it shot me into this entrepreneurial bliss.

Although that sounds quite catchy, it is not entirely true. See until I was about 25 years old, I had not saved, cared about saving, knew how to save or manage any type of money whatsoever. I was getting cash or let me rephrase the girl was with was getting cash and I was spending it. Didn't feel like much of a man at the time but I was having fun living my best life as they call it or so I thought.

A habit can form much faster than you can create it, and I had formed a habit of doing the wrong things. You know, following the wrong crowd, making all the wrong choices, going down the wrong path. If you ask me, I blame it on guidance, I do not remember having that role model in my life to show me what was possible. I was the type to think I could make anything possible and early on I started to truly believe that. Although being in a bad place and doing what I thought was all the wrong things, I made a promise to myself that I wanted better and to do that I had to make some changes.

The first one I started was I had to shift my thinking a bit. Being in the environment I was in it only required me to have one interest and I fell in love with that one interest and started to chase it. For me, money became the ultimate motive and I was always open to the next biggest and brightest idea that would grant me that entrepreneurial bliss I spoke about earlier. The thing about all of that, which most people miss nowadays, is there was an actual process and that process does not happen overnight.

There is no such thing as going from good to great unless you follow the process to get there. Think about any athlete, actor, and musician before they got to where they are now, they first had to start somewhere. Well, I wanted to get somewhere and that somewhere was in a better financial position.

As a young father, you are not thinking processes I was thinking more along the lines of how can I feed my sons, myself, and survive. This was around the time when I said personal development got into me. I knew a change was needed and that is what I did. I sought out the information, I put myself around other successful people, I developed new habits, I was doing everything I could think to do to get some money.

Even though I was personally developing, I remained focused on the one thing we tend to think will be the problem solver. The MONEY! Don't get me wrong you need money to provide and run a business and survive but it shouldn't be the sole focus of why you want your life to improve. I'm still developing now, and I've been at it for almost 10 years. It's a process as are many things in our lives if we took a second to look at them.

From birth to age 36, it was a process. From warehouse worker to assistant account executive that was a process. From running the streets to running a business. That was a process. See all parts of the process are needed and the results that come from that are usually money.

You also become a different person though and I can see that as well as others who have told me they have seen a change in not only my attitude but my approach toward life. You can change your life by just looking at things differently. By getting involved in different circles and being around some very successful people and just listening I saw firsthand that successful people think differently. Yes, they made money, but it was as a result of the people they became, and they did that by way of personal development.

I'm constantly developing, even now and I wanted to put everything I learned in a book to share it with someone else. To me, that is the best way to learn something it has been the very reason I've succeeded at things I'd never thought I accomplish. The statement serves true that "if I can do it so can you" take a second and think of a time where you did something that just outright amazed you, what was that feeling like? While remembering that feeling, think exactly about how you did it. Now as your telling someone else who is in the same position as you where how to improve and progress you finish it off by saying if I can do it so can you. Because it's true we all have special abilities and the thought of doing something great with your life has 99% of the time already been done so thinking of the statement now, can you see the truth behind it?

What would a "successful you" look like? The mind is so powerful to be able to turn a thought into things. I never really grasped the concept of that until I was late in life.

We always hear about do not waste time, but if it takes time for me to grow into who I need to be, then I would not say I'm necessarily wasting it. I've been embracing it as we all should, time is that factor that hinders some but grows others. I used to worry myself to death thinking the thought we all think when is it going to be my time? When was all the hard work going to pay off? When would my struggles end?

If you are reading any of these and nodding your head in the process, then I take it you know exactly where I was in my head. They say time can be your best friend or your worst enemy. I know time to be the very thing people take for granted, including me. I honestly can say I did not always make the best use of it; I'll admit procrastination is one of my flaws. I can remember back in my network marketing days I would go out to these events and always hear the top reps being asked the same question how long does it take? I'm assuming they mean to be successful; how long does that take? The answer was always, "Until...until either you're successful, you make it, or you get what you feel you deserve."

Do you feel like you have gotten what you deserve in life? Do you feel as if you have made it? I do not believe there is such a thing as "I've made it". Yeah, we can tell from where we started to where we are currently but there is always another level we have not yet reached.

In the process of doing so here is what I found to be true to reach that next level. There are not only certain skills and a level of confidence you must encompass, but there is also this inner person you must tap into and become because the saying remains true that "what got you here won't get you there". As I continued to better myself daily I started to look back at the little successes I had along the way and started putting together exactly what I did to accomplish those things like the awards, the trophies, the promotions and I laid it all out in this book.

The secret to vitality is in your movement, having the power or ability to continue in existence, a strong capacity for survival. With this guide, you now have a starting point.

CHAPTER 4

(In order to carry a positive action, we must develop a positive vision. – Dalai Lama)

The very starting point and the overall reason behind why this book came about have everything to do with the first step which I'll be sharing with you shortly. First, I want to ask you a question, what's that one reoccurring thought that you continuously keep having over and over and over again? Does it have anything to do with everlasting fame and riches? Or maybe it's about traveling the world and marrying the person of your dreams, or perhaps it's just about being able to make your family proud. Whatever it is, I'll share this piece of advice with you that someone kindly shared with me, if God brought you to it, then there's room for you to do it. I never knew the power of what I was capable of when it came to manifesting something into my life.

At some point or another, we have all had that idea that we thought was the one. I think I've had several, but it wasn't until I put things in perspective and gave the first step of this process a try. I know you're wondering what the v stands for well here it goes...visualization. I'm sure you've heard the saying before "thoughts become things," there's so much power in that statement alone. Here is why. When I was about 12 years old a lady named Ms. Helen would watch me and my sister while my mom went to school at night. While doing so she would always tell me the entire time boy you're in the wrong business, you need to be entertaining people.

As a child I was what you would call a jokester, I enjoyed making people laugh. Whether it was dancing, acting out something from a movie, or just being silly I was always entertaining and when company came over it never failed my mom hit me with her favorite line "Andre show them that little thing you do." The reality of what Ms. Helen had been telling me for all those years was starting to sink in; I just kind of kept it in the back of my mind though.

As I got older, never really losing my knack for entertaining I started to develop different passions and talents that I soon turned my attention towards. After coming home from college, I started hanging out with some guys who were doing music. I'd always been a fan of music, I could recite some of the hardest lines known to man from artists like Jay-Z, Biggie, Busta Rhymes, UGK, but when it came to me putting together music myself, I was like the worst of the worst. I had never even written a rap before let alone performed in public, but I wanted to be part of what these guys were doing so I got involved. Who would have known that I would take such a liking to this newfound talent, I wrote verses all day every day and even got to the point where I was putting my CDs together alone. Still following the advice Ms. Helen had told me years earlier I found myself still being an entertainer, but now from the stage as a motivational speaker.

The very thing that was implanted in my mind years ago became the very reason why I am where I am today. The thing I'm referencing; which is also the first step of this process is allowing yourself to visualize a vision. When I talk about a vision, I do not mean a random idea that we have now and then, or some little dream that we tell everyone about but never act on. No, I'm talking about a clear, concise, open visualization of that very thing in life you said you wanted. I need to know what it feels like to be walking in our dream, what it looks like to be living that dream, what does it taste like, what does it sound like. I need to be able to embrace your vision as you talk about to the point where I can imagine it. That is the type of vision I'm talking about.

Are you envisioning your life that way? There is a quote by Jonathan Swift that reads "vision is the art of seeing what is invisible to others" meaning your vision is your vision, it was given to you for a reason and rather than us bring that vision to life we tend to allow others to cast their vision for our own lives. I'll admit I'm guilty of it, we're all guilty of it, the way we defend ourselves against it though are the same steps outlined in this book. When was the last time you had a clear visualization about something you wanted in life? Did you get it? If so, what was the feeling like afterwards, knowing that you could manifest something just by focusing your mind and turning your energy towards it?

I can remember just reveling at how much fun we would have at the gym after school, which was the meeting spot for me and the guys. There was not much going on to do anything else but play sports. My choice was always basketball, but I did not get serious until the 1996 draft and I watched Allen Iverson walk across the stage. That moment did two things for me, 1 it made me feel proud to be from Virginia and 2 it allowed me to cast a vision about what I wanted to do and the possibility of it happening.

It is easy to want something; the not so easy part is bringing yourself to fight for it. There was not a lot of people that get a chance to go pro, and if you do, you're damn good. The only thing that stops us and stopped me was the belief that I was just that good. Day in and day out every minute I had to practice if I wasn't at the court, I would be downstairs in my mom's basement just dribbling. Working on my left hand, working on my right hand, working on my crossover you name it. Other guys in the neighborhood were starting to see a difference in my game and the praise I got helped my confidence in believing I was good or at least getting better. I started to envision myself playing ball for my school, maybe college, I mean who knows the sky is the limit right...all this newfound excitement abruptly came to an end.

My ninth-grade year after putting on a show during tryouts and just giving it everything I had I didn't make the team. I was devastated, but after seeing the same thing happen in tenth grade made me question things. You can just about imagine where my belief was now for that vision. It has been said that life is going to test you at times to see if what you said you wanted is really what you meant. I wanted to play basketball, I wanted to go pro but in reality, I know the odds of having that happen, and it was that little seed of doubt that pushed me to not only lose confidence in that vision it also made me turn away from the focus I had on basketball.

A solid belief in the vision that you have for your life and seeing the end game and living it out before ever even obtaining it is the part of living V.I.T.A.L that takes some work. It is you coming out of your comfort zone and letting go of any what ifs. If I was ever going to put this book together, I had to take my advice and let go of the fear of not believing that I could be an author and not only impact people from the stage but through a book. By now I hope you have a clear idea of something you are going to commit to working towards. Also make sure that idea is put somewhere that you can see it every day, if you go back and think about when you were asked in elementary what you wanted to be when you grow up, your answer usually came from something that you saw and after seeing it you started to see it more and more to the point you took a liking to it and started to visualize yourself doing it. So, by the time the teacher asked you it was already on the frontal lobe of your mind. That type of visualization is what we must get back to, we have already experienced living V.I.T.A.L at a young age but now is when we have the power to follow through and make it a reality. Are you ready?

-Describe your ideal life in great detail from beginning to end (what it looks like, what it feels like, what you're driving, where your living, who your friends are etc.)

-What are 3 things you can do today to start walking in your vision? (write them down and add it into your routine every day)

-Share your vision with 3 friends that have known and supported you.

CHAPTER 5

(Live less out of habit and more out of intent – Amy Rubin Flett)

There is a great power we all possess; it has been described as the ability to manifest and attract what we want into our lives. It's almost like drawing a map of where you want to go and in doing so it allows you to focus on who you are in the moment. This power I'm referring to, if practiced daily, can change your life. Now, I'm sure you've heard that before but here's where things differ. I'm not suggesting you set another goal; although they are very helpful to your success; what I'm talking about is setting your intentions.

An intention is an idea that you plan or intend to carry out. Whether you pull it off or not, it is something you mean to do. Every day I wake up I repeat to myself that I have every intention of becoming a successful speaker, I then ignite on that intention by taking action to do so. Once you visualize what truly want for your life you then begin taking the necessary steps towards it and you will see that your intention determines your outcome. If you are not already feeling a spark or some type of excitement, then I encourage you to keep reading. In this chapter we will dive into just how effective this part of the process can be, it is what I like to call igniting your intention.

We just took some time to truly outline and understand how to visualize a clear precise vision for ourselves, I hope you followed along and took the time to go through the steps and wrote out your vision. The question now becomes how do I move forward towards that vision? You may want to start by asking a more specific question, what initially made me choose this path and want to achieve such a vision in the first place? Was it only fueled by money, or do you have a deep desire to make an impact and leave your mark on the world? These questions never really came to mind for me at first, I just knew I wanted to be free of having to get up and go to work every day to a job I despised and not have to live life on someone else's terms other than my own. I figured the only way to make that happen is to become financially free. So, my path was mainly fueled by money because my belief at that time was this is the solution. But as with everything in our lives we are always subject to change.

You need to know that your vision is powered by a particular process and I found that to be very true taking part in all the business opportunities I started and stopped throughout the years. I'd be so committed to my new venture running off pure excitement for about the first 6 months or so and right around that seventh or eighth month sometime a little longer if there weren't any results that I felt comfortable with. That very same excitement I once had begun to fade, and my attention would slowly start to turn towards something else. This continued for a few years until I realized I had only cast a vision which I never wrote down but more importantly I was not laser-focused on stepping into that vision by backing it with an intention statement.

The more we write things down and read over them daily the more our minds begin to create that as our reality. I would hear people say all the time how important it was to write down your goals and write out your vision for your life but I wanted to do things my way and maybe that's exactly where you are right now, so I'll ask you this question "How's that been working out for you?"

Upon starting my journey in the area of speaking, I had no idea of the direction I wanted to go I just knew I wanted to learn how to be a better speaker that would inspire thousands like I've seen people like Les Brown and Eric Thomas do. Of course, you don't wake up one day and just become a world speaker; these guys have spent years practicing and studying to perfect their craft in a way that they created a lane for themselves in a now very crowded space. After doing some deep research and looking at my own life in comparison, I found some similarities. We all have an extremely powerful story that has affected our lives in some way. We all have a targeted audience of people we speak too but the differences between us is what stood out the most. And no, it was not just the money aspect. It was something much more obvious; I had no intention statement.

What was I going to ignite on? Many of us have developed a habit of taking activity as an accomplishment and that is not the case. It is not benefiting you to just be busy. There has to be a direct purpose in mind when bringing your vision to reality. The steps needed to do that come straight from your intention statement. The understanding came once I realized the intention statement was more than just words. Having to sit down and write it out pushed me outside of my comfort zone because it made me think about "who I am". However, at this point I was committed to doing something different and here is what I came up with.

"I am committed to being an awesome dad, friend, and leader who blesses family, friends, and people I meet with creative solutions that inspire a belief in them to make the switch from living an ordinary life to an extraordinary one.

I intend to inspire, innovate, and lead young males to become the future leaders and fathers of tomorrow, ensuring them that no matter your circumstances you have the power to live the life you desire.

I attract people who I can best serve with my message of living V.I.T.A.L and with whom I can assist in helping them grow towards success. I am surrounded by positive influential brothers and sisters that are committed to living the core 4 and being the best version of themselves."

Sounds pretty good, right? It was interesting after writing this; I came to find out what drove me to become better. Do you have a belief that you deserve the type of life you want to create? Because if you do; then it is that same belief that will fuel your intention to stay ignited. I encourage you after reading this chapter to find out what gives you the most joy and see if you can capture that in writing your intention statement. As you read these words aloud and speak them out with conviction, they will become you and start to create some momentum in your life as you continue your journey through the process. What comes next is a very important part of living V.I.T.A.L but before we jump into that

Let's get you ignited: Here's how you start:

---After writing out your vision, write your intent statement. When doing so ask yourself this question: what is it I hope to bring to the world? (Read both vision and intent statement aloud each day)

---Helping people is a part of who you are. Connect with one to two organizations within the alignment of your vision so that you may offer your time and attention to and put it on your calendar.

---Get committed to continuous learning. Piece of advice though, do not learn anything new before implementing what was previously learned.

CHAPTER 6

(The best mindset is to be unafraid. – Malcolm Gladwell)

I have a divine love for reading. I believe some of the best information for obtaining success is found in the books you read. I was recently reading one titled "The Greatest Salesman in the World," written by great American author Og Mandino. In this book, there was a passage that said: "Failure will never overtake me if my determination to succeed is strong enough". I knew right then that, no matter what I was up against or what was coming my way, there was no other option but to take control of my destiny and press on to live my dreams. That statement alone can justify the importance of the next phase of this process simply because it's the fear of failure or the fear of not doing something right that keeps us from not doing anything at all. Learning to train yourself to be unafraid could be that mental shift needed to take you from where you are to where you want to go, but as some would say "sounds easier said than done".

I never understood why people made success such a scary thing. Every single day a new entrepreneur is emerging, doing something remarkable to provide and leave a legacy for their family. The one thing that separates them from us is the belief that they deserve it; backed by a "will not" quit attitude. Let's face it; if you don't accept failure then there may be no hope for you. Our successes and our failures are where we gain the most experience, some of the greatest success stories came to be because of failures.

Most just won't do what it requires you to, so I think it's time we release some of those old behaviors that are no longer working. I was a big advocate of the phrase "I have always been this way" until I recognized that it was the problem. I'm still learning about this part of the process myself, facing some of my failures, I've learned a few key points that have been able to keep me in the game.

When experiencing any type of success even the smallest accomplishment can make way for your ego to be filled and make you think that you've reached a pivotal point and you can start to let up. It's very easy to have this happen. I know personally because this was exactly what I was going through days before attending my first toastmaster's event. Coming into toastmasters I hit the ground running right away. I was so excited to qualify to compete in the international speech contest. My speech about bullying had garnered the attention of some of the members and they encouraged me to compete. I won at the club level and advanced to the area level where the competition was a lot tougher. I went up against some very dynamic speakers and this was my first time doing something like this.

Toastmasters gives you a manual on how to put a speech together, but I didn't know much about speech writing or presenting in a way that captures and holds an audience's attention. I figured I would continue with the same speech and present it the same way I had been doing all this time. Here is a little secret I'll pass on to you: there's truth in the phrase "what got you here won't get you there" and I'm a living example of that.

It is two days before the competition and I finally find out who my opponents are. The fact that I know two out of the four competitors, because I have previously heard them speak, I began to start doubting myself by thinking "could I win this thing"? The 4th opponent was a member of a club not too far away from mine, but it was a name I had not heard before, Wendy Moon. She had been a toastmaster for quite some time, but I never saw her in action.

Pumping myself up and listening to what others were telling me I started to ease up like I had this thing in the bag. I became very relaxed in my preparation to make sure my speech was solid. Even though I knew it and could recite every word perfectly, there were still some tweaks that could have made it better. It is finally the day of the contest and usually, I'm a little bit anxious right before I speak but this particular day, I'm feeling great. I'm dressed like a winner, not to mention I have friends and family in the audience to cheer me on.

As I start to scan the room, I see the chairs starting to fill up. It's almost show-time. They gather all of us together and go over the debriefing for the contest. Upon picking cards to see our speaking order, guess who draws lucky number 1? No sweat. I've got this in the bag, remember? As I make my way to the stage the host is wrapping up my wonderful introduction. I take my place and with all eyes, on me, I pause for just a second as I raise my head and began to speak. I don't utter a word, not a noise, not a cough, absolutely nothing.

Talk about embarrassed, all the preparation I had done and excitement I had leading up to this very moment and when it counted most I froze. I had forgotten my lines! I'm sitting there in front of this audience in dead silence. I stood there for about a minute and a half before I regained my train of thought and started to tell my story. However, it was nothing like how I had planned it and I was not impressed with any of it. All I kept thinking was "way to go Andre good luck setting the tone with that performance".

After watching the other contestants give their speeches, I felt more and more disappointed with myself, knowing that I could have won if I'd taken it more seriously. When the judges came back with their ballots it was no question who had won, you guessed it, Wendy Moon. That day was a real harsh reality lesson for me to show that we can never let our past successes allow us to think we are so far along that we let up from doing the things necessary to keep progressing.

Training yourself to be unafraid does not have to be all about facing your fears. It can also be about getting comfortable with the uncomfortable. I find this to be a hard task as well. The more comfortable we get with something the harder it is for us to break away from it. Sometimes it's the smallest thing. I used to have this habit of ordering the same thing no matter the restaurant. Just about every menu has a chicken alfredo dish and that was my meal of choice every time. It was not until I got uncomfortable and tried something different did, I realize what I had been missing out on.

Where have you gotten comfortable or complacent in your life? If you were to get uncomfortable and take a new approach how much further do you think you could go? I learned this is just another stage of fear and if we live in fear then we never step out and take risks.

My risk was writing this manifesto in fear of how it would be received. Knowing this is not for everyone I wrote it, anyway, living V.I.T.A.L allowed me to find the confidence needed. So, I share with you this: train yourself to be unafraid. Be unafraid of the unknown, be unafraid of those who think differently or do not support you, be unafraid of failure, be unafraid to take risks and most importantly be unafraid to be yourself. Here are some ways to help you get started:

Write down 3 principles you live by.

Name 3 reasons why you deserve better than what you are currently getting.

What is one thing you have trained yourself to be unafraid of?

CHAPTER 7

(Authenticity is your most precious commodity as a leader. –Marcus Buckingham)

I was speaking with a friend of mine the other day. I'm subtly eavesdropping on the conversation behind us, to the point I've tuned my friend out. It was because I heard something that caught my attention. It was said that the worst feeling in the world is being uncomfortable in YOUR skin. Is that true?

I'm sure there's a point in our lives where we just don't feel like ourselves sometimes. Trust me I've had those days, but the key is to learn how to feel comfortable. Understand that by doing so you become more accepting of your true self. One of the easiest things to do in the world today is to be you. With the love of simplicity in today's society for some this has become a major challenge. There is great courage in being who you are and for that reason this part of the process is extremely important. If you have made it this far, I suspect you have seen a slight change in how you think and definitely how you feel.

While writing this I was reminded of a time when I was growing up wanting to be this famous athlete like the ones I would watch on TV. Even in school when the teacher would ask me what I wanted to be; my answer was always the same; a famous athlete. You would hear other kids yell out these different professions, a cop, a firefighter, a doctor but did they envision themselves being that person or was it just based on something they saw?

Have we been taught from an early age to be copies of other people instead of just being ourselves? I would hope not. However, we see as time passes that what we wanted to be growing up will change numerous times. As our desire grows to become the leaders of our lives, we find that becoming authentic is more of an individual mission that most are still traveling. There is an upside to that! That is: there is so much more to you that has not been tapped into yet.

I was reading this quote by a guy they call the Daily Motivator who goes by the name Ralph Marston. I simply just love quotes because they are so relatable to what I'm going through in my life at that time. Here's what that quote said, "the greatest accomplishment in the world is BEING YOU in a world that's constantly trying to make you something else". To be authentic is to know one's self. So, I ask "Who are you?"

I battled with the answer to that question many times over. I did not have an idea of who I was. I felt I knew what I liked but when it came down to it, I did not know how to be vulnerable. Asking me this question back then would have gotten you the answer of "I'm Andre St. George" and that is probably about as far as it would have gone. I could not tell you what I was passionate about or what I felt I was good at. I always found myself following what I thought everyone else thought was cool.

What about what I thought? It's almost like I didn't have a voice, and for years I traveled this cycle. There is a point in life where you are going to feel lost. I had reached that point only because I hadn't identified who I was yet. It felt as if I had taken on a new identity at times. It is so easy being like someone else and I believe this is the sole reason the world is full of fakes. Now, we as a society have this superficial look on the word REAL. We despise those who do not wear, act, or do real things. But when was the last time you saw or heard anyone take a look in the mirror and ask themselves: Why am I not being authentic?

Authenticity requires a genuine sharing of one's inner self. You know, that place most people are not willing to tap into due to the fear of being exposed. With the fear of judgment one can be limited to being honest or even vulnerable with themselves or others.

I've had this hindrance plague me in own life in relationships, friendships, and other interactions many times over. But it required me to develop this measure of personal authenticity and I discovered that by simply changing what I said to myself. Sounds pretty easy right? The simplest changes usually are and for you to be more authentic that will usually be the place where you start. I remembered hearing this speaker say that at an event one time. What was significant about that was the question the speaker asked. No matter how many different ways I looked at it for the life of me I could not come up with a reasonable enough answer that would justify my response. He proceeded to ask the audience "How Many Times?" and it was almost like it was echoing as I heard it over and over again in my head.

How many times, have you consistently looked in the mirror at yourself and told YOU, as he pointed his finger to a different person in the audience each time, that I'm a WINNER! He asked the question with so much conviction and passion that I sat up in my seat as if that was going to make me him any clearer. What it did was lit a fuse that got the gears turning because I knew in the past, I've looked into that mirror a few times said those words but never consistently.

I'll be honest some days I don't particularly like the person that's looking back at me but it's those times when I should be telling myself I'm A Winner the most. Just as everyone in the audience was hanging onto his every word, right there from center stage he starts reciting his mantra for dealing with not being his true authentic self. "No matter what I've been through, I'm here because I'm a winner!" "No matter if they approve of me, I'm not scared because

I'm a winner!" "No matter if they say I can't, I can, I will because I'm a winner." It was at that moment I understood the real importance behind what we tell ourselves and why it should be done consistently.

I felt like I was a winner sitting in that audience, the energy you felt in that room made you just want to jump out your seat. I was supposed to hear that message because even to this day I'm very mindful of the conversations I have with myself. It requires me to live with more conviction. To be honest, there is no better way to invite more grace, gratitude and joy into your life than by being authentic.

The authentic you give off a more confident feeling, thus forming more authentic relationships and allows the making for more authentic decisions. I hope by now you are thinking of your own life and how authenticity can help redefine your values so that you may realize and understand your true self. The 4th step to living V.I.T.A.L is as important as the first, second and third.

While writing this I thought to myself if this book was to help anyone this part of the process would be key in their development. Let us continue to allow our true selves to be seen. Here are some questions to help you get started:

If you knew me, would you know this?

What is one thing others assume about you that you wish were true?

Do you sometimes feel afraid of people knowing who you truly are? If so, explain why?

CHAPTER 8

(If you do what you love, you'll never work a day in your life. –Marc Anthony)

A life worth living is a life worth loving. Or maybe it's a life worth recording, something to that effect, I'm not quite sure. I want to congratulate you for making it this far, you have reached the final part of the process and I can guess by now you have an idea what the "L" must stand for. In case you haven't figured it out yet allow me to tell you. It is the great motivator. It is the very thing that keeps us pursing that next level in life or that next success. It is that thing that when you take away all the money you still perform to the best of your ability. If you have followed the rest of the principals up until this point, then I know you are already living V.I.T.A.L because you love what you do. The "L" stands for love. We must love what we do, we must love who we are, and we must love the process. If so, there is no doubt you will love the reward.

You are probably thinking like I was when I first took a look at this, "why is the easiest thing to do the very last principal?" I thought about it ...having to visualize a true vision for yourself is not the easiest thing if you do not have an idea about what you are passionate about, but it is doable. Then you experience the igniting of your intention and this gets you going! It gets the momentum moving and you see things start to form. For me learning how to say no to procrastination and yes to production was my turning point.

From there you go right into the A, which is my favorite and that stands for authentic, being, doing, living authentically. Once you develop an understanding of your true self the vision becomes much clearer and in doing so we learn to not play the comparison game because we all have our paths to follow. Then there is the L, love what you do. I do not think I can say it any simpler than that. I guess I can see why you would consider this the easiest part of the process, but I think figuratively it is the most required.

Having a passion for something is one thing but loving what you do is the ultimate accomplishment. There were times when I thought I loved what I did but soon found out that I only liked it. Upon moving to the Westside of Atlanta I was fortunate enough to catch that relatively popular music bug. A few friends I'd been hanging out with started a rap group. They were pretty known in the area. It is a very true statement that you are the sum of the people you hang around most. In my case, I was the prime example. I'd never recorded myself before, much less ever wrote a rhyme. I did not know how to count bars. Music was just something I never pictured myself doing and here I am sitting in the studio with these guys about to drop a song. It was scary but exciting. They did not know I couldn't rap, and I sure wasn't going to tell them. What happened was they welcomed me, and I believe that is what gave me life, that belief.

There are times when we do not think others believe in us and we stop believing ourselves. Not this time though. I always had a respect for music. I love the art and who doesn't appreciate a good song? To now be doing it was key and there was no chance I was going to let this opportunity pass me by. The more I got a chance to record, the more I wanted to write, the more I wanted to perform, the more I became a part of it. I was accepted by people I had never met; women I would have probably never talked to. The excitement of it all was addictive.

There is this unexplainable feeling you get when you are performing in front of a crowd of people especially our peers and they're reciting every word right along with you. It wasn't so much that we made any money from it all, it was more so the experience and fame that came as a result. I even had the opportunity of sitting amongst other famous artists like Shawty Lo, TI, Fabo just to name a few and being around when they created some of the music we listen to today. I was living a dream that others longed for but as we all know every good thing eventually comes to an end and the high you once felt has now become a surprising low.

If you have any idea how the music biz operates then you can understand that it takes a minute for the money to come unless you previously had it before coming in, or you are fortunate enough to write a hit song. For me, it was neither and for many artists today (new or old) it is the same cycle because the vision is tainted. It's not so much for the love of it anymore but more about the money and fame we glamorize within it.

I was only a part of the group. I didn't necessarily start with them so there wasn't much coming my way. I survived off of living with my girlfriend at the time and working a warehouse job to get by. I was still out at the clubs and seen hanging out with the guys, but the music had fallen to the waist side and became secondary!

What I did not know was when you stop doing something after being in full momentum of it makes it harder to just come back and pick it up. Your interest is not the same, your attention is now elsewhere, and you now find out that what you thought you loved doing was only something you liked. Although I still dabbled in it from time to time, I concluded that I just liked music. It was made clear. Maybe you can agree that when you love what you do you find a way to stay at it despite the obstacles, the setbacks, the non-believers, and everything else that is going to come at you while you're moving forward.

Let's test it out...take a second and think about something in your life that you love to do. Now tell me, has it always been easy to do? Nope probably not, but I bet you stayed at it because you loved what you were doing. When you just like something it is easy to give it up and quit and try something else. When you love something, you will see it through to the end. This can be said with anything in your life if you love what you do the dedication you have towards it is remarkable.

I hope you have given some real thought to how a few tweaks in how you think and how you operate can help propel your life in a new direction. I love being able to inspire people because it is a gift that I was given that has always been with me I just never took the time to cultivate it. Starting SGS Solutions and being a mentor for young males facing some of the hardships today that I faced when I was their age has been a trajectory to the path that was created for me. Whether it was inspiring those with a message through my music or now being able to inspire those with a message of strength and confidence through speaking, I now have a foothold on where I'm most passionate and my vision is clear.

As we round out the last part of the process, I ask you this question: did adding these principles to your life help you to improve in any area? If so, I challenge you to continuously add all parts of these principles until the V.I.T.A.L method becomes a pivotal part of your life. Here are some questions you can ask yourself to keep you accountable:

Can you describe in detail why do you do what you do?

If there was no public recognition or significant financial benefit would you still do it?

What are you telling yourself and others about who you are and what is important to you?

If there is a small amount of evidence that your fears or limiting beliefs might come to pass, is the risk big enough to prevent you from going after what you love to do?

CHAPTER 9

At the end of the day we all choose to believe what we think to be true and that shapes how we live our lives. Before I started waking up at 5 a.m. every morning I would lay there in bed up until the very last minute then get up and rush to get myself together to go out and take on the day. That resulted in me developing a habit of lateness and low self-discipline because my mind was not strong enough to tell my body that its time "let's move!"

I have since learned that the early morning hours for me are the best time because whatever I went to sleep with, I can now filter out and during my workouts, I can put in something motivational that gives me a clear fresh start for the day ahead. For you, this could be in the afternoon or you may feel more complete releasing the clutter and everything from your mind at night. Whichever it is, do what works best. However, at some point to shift into that V.I.T.A.L stage of your life and do what's necessary, we must believe that it is the minor distractions that keep us from focusing on what we want to accomplish.

It is the negative belief or private conversations that we have with ourselves that stall us from reaching that success plateau that has already been designed for us. If you could take what I just outlined in the earlier chapters of this book and start to apply it to one thing in your life, what would that be? After breaking down mentally, facing adversity, and discovering who I was I came to realize everything I went through was all a part of my survival to get where I am today. The phrase living V.I.T.A.L has always been instilled in me since the beginning and for that very reason, I have not quit.

If you are reading this and you have not given up either, then living V.I.T.A.L is a part of you as well because you have survived through whatever obstacles have plagued you or tried to take you away from being the person you needed to be. It is never OK to just be OK and no one should ever become comfortable living life just OK. You are destined for so much more in life and the V.I.T.A.L method can help you get there as it has done for me and others. I hope you enjoy.

About the Author

Andre St. George resides in Newport News, Virginia, where he is a youth educator and entrepreneur. His brand's message is, "empowerment and belief in one's potential." Andre focuses are raising future leaders and community involvement. Andre's passion is encouraging people to go after what they desire in life.

4-U-Nique Publishing

Read excerpts, get exclusive inside looks at exciting new titles and authors, find tour schedules and enter contests.

www.4-U-NiquePublishing.com

Need help publishing your masterpiece? We are happy to help.

Email us at info@4-U-NiquePublishing.com

www.ingramcontent.com/pod-product-compliance
Lightning Source LLC
Chambersburg PA
CBHW070818170726
48000CB00018B/1239